Super Science
Turned On by
Electricity

by Elise Richards
Illustrations by J. Angel

Troll

Printed in the United States of America.
ISBN 0-8167-4254-5

10 9 8 7 6 5 4 3 2 1

Contents

Introduction 3

What Is Electricity? 4

Static Electricity 5

Experiment #1: Leaping Pepper **6**

Experiment #2: Electricity in a Jar **7**

Current Electricity 8

Generating Current 9

Experiment #3: Lemon Battery..**10**

Experiment #4: All Lit Up **11**

Traveling the Circuit...12

Experiment #5: Make a Switch **13**

Conductivity 14

Experiment #6: Complete the Circuit **15**

Resistance 16

Experiment #7: Make a Rheostat **17**

Electrical Heat and Light...18

Experiment #8: Sparks in the Dark..................................**19**

Series and Parallel 20

Experiment #9: Brighter and Dimmer **21**

Electricity and Magnetism..22

Experiment #10: Go with the Flow **23**

Electricity and You..24

⚡ IMPORTANT ELECTRICAL SAFETY INFORMATION ⚡

- *Never insert anything other than an electrical plug into a wall outlet. The power from a wall outlet is strong enough to kill you if handled incorrectly.*
- *Never handle electricity from an outlet or electrical appliances plugged into an outlet when your hands are wet. You could receive a powerful electrical shock.*
- *As you do the experiments in this book, be very careful handling wires when they are connected to a battery—they can become quite hot.*
- *Disconnect all wires from your battery when you are finished experimenting. Unattended wires can create a serious fire hazard.*

Introduction

Electricity is one of the most powerful forces in nature. The brilliant flashes of lightning that crackle down from the sky during a thunderstorm are raw electrical power, strong enough to kill. But harnessed, electricity is one of our greatest helpers. Electrical power generated by machines turns on our lights, powers our computers, cooks our food, runs our televisions and stereos, and does thousands of other things that affect our lives each and every day.

With *Turned On by Electricity*, you'll learn all about electricity. The easy experiments in this book will show you how to make a battery out of a lemon and how to produce sparks in a jar. You'll also make pepper leap off a table without touching it, cause a bulb to burst into brilliant life, and much more!

This kit includes most of the things you will need to explore the exciting world of electricity:

TIPS

1. Good scientists always set up their labs before they begin their experiments. Make sure that you have gathered all the materials you need before you start an experiment. Also, note that some experiments in this book require an adult's help.

2. If your experiment doesn't work the first time, try it again. Check to make sure your wires are connected correctly and firmly. Loose connections are the most common cause of experiment failure. Also, if your results aren't as described in this book, try to figure out what happened.

3. Write down the results of your experiments so you can answer any questions that may arise later. Who knows…maybe you will make a new discovery!

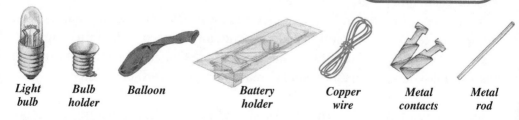

| Light bulb | Bulb holder | Balloon | Battery holder | Copper wire | Metal contacts | Metal rod |

Other materials needed for the experiments, such as a lemon, tape, D-cell batteries, cardboard, pepper, and pencils, can be found in your home or at a craft-supply or grocery store.

What Is Electricity?

Electricity is a form of energy that is based on a very simple natural principle, the principle that *positive and negative charges attract each other.* Every object you see contains both positive and negative particles, so this natural attraction is going on all the time.

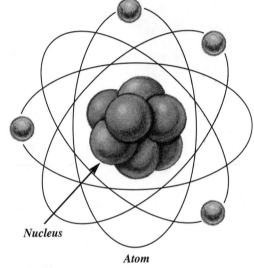

Nucleus

Atom

Electricity begins with *atoms*—incredibly small particles that make up everything around us. As tiny as they are, atoms are made up of even smaller particles called *protons, neutrons,* and *electrons.* Protons carry a positive charge, electrons carry a negative charge, and neutrons carry no charge. The protons and neutrons are found at the atom's center in a dense cluster known as the *nucleus.* The electrons whirl around the nucleus at very high speeds, forming a kind of outer "shell."

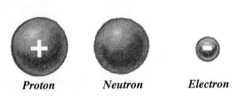

Proton   Neutron   Electron

An atom usually has the same number of protons as electrons, so the positive and negative charges cancel each other out. This means that an atom in its natural state is electrically *neutral* (it has no charge). But atoms can gain or lose electrons and become unbalanced. When this happens, the electrons move rapidly from one atom to another in an attempt to restore the natural balance. This movement creates, or *generates*, electricity.

There are two types of electricity: *static* and *current.* Static electricity occurs in one spot; current electricity is in constant motion.

Static Electricity

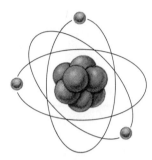

Positive ion

You have seen that electrons can move from one atom to another. When an atom gains or loses electrons, its balance is upset, and the atom has an electrical charge. An atom that carries either a positive or a negative charge is called an *ion*.

Normally, an ion would try to neutralize itself by taking on or releasing electrons. But it can't do this if there are no oppositely charged ions around. In this situation, the ion must carry the charge, remaining in an unbalanced state. Static electricity builds up when many ions gather together.

Negative ion

Static electricity can be found anywhere. You have probably noticed some of your shirts and socks sticking together when they come out of the dryer, or heard your hair crackle as you comb it. That's static electricity at work. And let's not forget lightning, the most spectacular display of electricity in nature. It takes countless billions of ions to produce enough static electricity for just one lightning strike!

The experiments on the next two pages let you explore some fascinating effects of static electricity. But note that it can be difficult to generate static electricity if the air where you live is very humid. If you have trouble making any of the experiments in this book work, find an air-conditioned room and try again.

Static electricity can make your clothes stick together in the dryer.

Experiment #1: Leaping Pepper

How can you generate enough static electricity to attract small objects?

Set-up

Prepare your lab:
- pepper shaker (filled with pepper)
- balloon*

*included in this kit

STEPS

1. Shake a few dashes of pepper onto a table.
2. Blow up the balloon and tie it closed. (Get an adult to help if you have trouble doing this.)
3. Rub the inflated balloon up and down the front of your shirt about ten times, or until you feel your shirt begin to stick to you. *(Hint: A flannel, wool, or silk shirt works best. A sweater works well also. If all else fails, rub the balloon briskly against some carpeting.)*
4. Hold the balloon 1 to 2 inches (2.5 to 5 cm) above the pepper. Move it back and forth. What happens?

Conclusion

When you rub the balloon on your shirt, you transfer electrons from your shirt to the balloon, creating ions and generating static electricity. The negative electrical force in the balloon attracts positive particles in the pepper, making it leap upward.

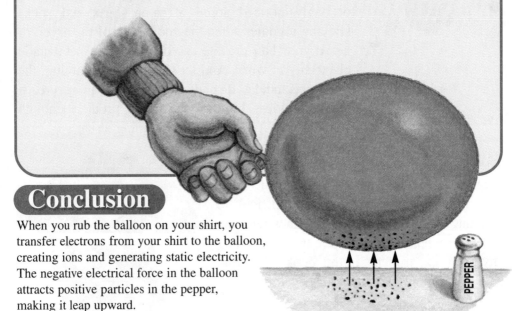

Experiment #2: Electricity in a Jar

Is it possible to store static electricity?

Set-up

Prepare your lab:
- one 5-inch by 2-inch (12.5-cm x 5-cm) strip of aluminum foil
- empty 35-mm film canister with lid
- cup with water
- ballpoint pen
- metal rod*
- the balloon you blew up for Experiment #1

*included in this kit

STEPS

1. Wrap the foil strip around the bottom half of the film canister, crumpling it to fit the shape of the canister.
2. With the lid off, pour water into the canister until it is about two-thirds full. Put the lid back on the canister.
3. Use the ballpoint pen to punch a hole in the lid. (Ask an adult to help if the canister you're using has a thick lid.) Insert the metal rod into the hole until only about ½ inch (1.25 cm) of the rod is left outside the canister. The rod should be partly submerged in the water.
4. Hold the canister in one hand, making sure you touch only the aluminum foil. With your other hand, hold the balloon. Rub the balloon against your shirt until an electrical charge builds up (see Experiment #1 for a list of the shirt fabrics that work best), then touch the balloon to the end of the metal rod.
5. Set the balloon down and touch the rod with the tip of your finger. What happens?
6. What happens if you do Step 4 two or three times before you touch the rod?

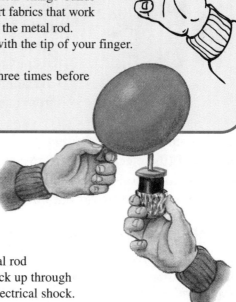

Balloon

Negative ions

Rod

Canister

Foil

Conclusion

Each time you touch the charged balloon to the metal rod, electrons travel down through the rod and into the water inside the canister. The more times you charge the water, the more electricity you store. When you touch the metal rod with your finger, the stored electrons travel back up through the rod into your body, and you feel a small electrical shock.

Current Electricity

Even though static electricity is very common in the natural world, it is not often put to work in our everyday lives. Instead, we use current electricity to light our lamps, run our TVs, play our stereos, and do just about anything else that requires electrical power. As its name suggests, current electricity occurs when many electrons flow together in a current. The movement of the electrons generates an electrical charge that continues for as long as the electrons continue to flow.

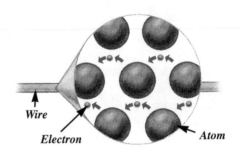

Electrons "leap" from one atom to the next as they travel in a current.

To understand current electricity, imagine you are crossing a stream by jumping from one rock to the next. The rocks don't move, but you can reach the opposite side of the stream by stepping on each rock in turn. Electrons move forward in a similar way. Just like the rocks in the stream, the atoms stay in one place. The electrons "leap" from one atom to the next as they travel.

Electrical current may be *direct* (the electrons travel in one direction only) or *alternating* (the electrons keep reversing direction). Direct current is usually called by its initials, *DC;* alternating current is called *AC*. Most of the electricity we use to power our homes is alternating current.

⚡ **WARNING:** *Alternating current, which comes out of the wall outlets in your home, is very powerful. Never insert anything other than an electrical plug into these outlets. Note that all the experiments in this book use a weak DC current that will not hurt you. However, a stronger DC current could harm you, so always take safety precautions when dealing with electricity from any power source.*

Generating Current

In order for electrons to flow in a current, they need a "push." That push is provided by a power source such as a battery or a generator. Batteries produce direct current (DC); most generators produce alternating current (AC).

Power sources generate electricity by creating both positive and negative ions. These ions gather at two terminals, one negative and one positive. When the terminals are connected in the proper way, the extra electrons from the negative terminal begin to move toward the positive terminal. This electron movement provides the push that keeps the current flowing.

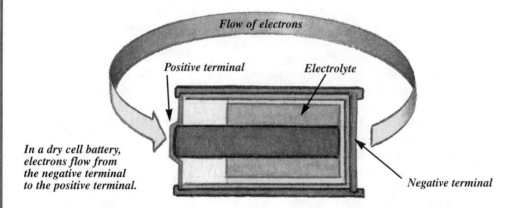

Flow of electrons

Positive terminal

Electrolyte

In a dry cell battery, electrons flow from the negative terminal to the positive terminal.

Negative terminal

Most of the experiments in this kit use a dry cell battery as the power source. In a regular dry cell battery, one terminal is made of zinc, the other of carbon. The terminals touch an electrolyte—a substance that sets off chemical reactions in the battery. During these reactions, positive ions build up in the carbon and negative ions build up in the zinc. A small electrical exchange occurs constantly within the battery, but electrons *really* begin to flow when the battery's terminals are connected on the outside to an electrical device, such as a flashlight or a tape player.

> ⚡ ***WARNING:*** *Never break open a battery. The electrolyte inside can give you a painful acid burn.*

Turned On by Electricity

Experiment #3: Lemon Battery

How do you turn a lemon into a battery?

Set-up · *Prepare your lab:*
- scissors
- copper wire*

- sandpaper
- penny
- lemon

- sharp knife
- metal rod*

*included in this kit

STEPS

1. Using the scissors, cut a 5-inch (12.5-cm) section of copper wire. Use the sandpaper to strip 1 inch (2.5 cm) of covering off one end of the wire and 3 inches (7.5 cm) off the other end.
2. Wrap the 3-inch (7.5-cm) stripped section around a penny several times, then twist it closed at the top to secure.
3. Roll the lemon firmly on a table, pressing down hard on it as you roll, to make the inside juicy. Then ask an adult to help you cut a slit in the side of the lemon with the knife. Insert the wrapped penny into the slit, leaving the wire hanging out.
4. Insert the metal rod into the lemon about 1 inch (2.5 cm) from where you inserted the penny. *Make sure the penny and the rod do not touch each other inside the lemon.*
5. Touch the stripped end of the wire and the tip of the rod to your tongue at the same time. What happens? Now touch your tongue to the rod and the wire separately. What happens this time?

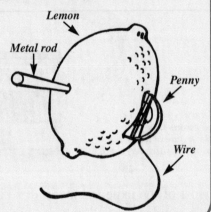

Lemon

Metal rod

Penny

Wire

Conclusion

The rod and the penny act as negative and positive terminals, respectively, and the lemon juice acts as an electrolyte. A very small electrical current is generated. When you touch the wire and the rod with your tongue at the same time, you taste a metallic flavor as the electricity stimulates your taste buds. When you touch the rod and the wire separately, no electricity flows, and there is no metallic taste.

> ⚡ **WARNING: This experiment is safe because the amount of electricity generated is very small. But as a rule you should never put electrical wires into your mouth!**

Experiment #4: All Lit Up

Can a single battery generate enough electrical current to light a bulb?

Set-up

Prepare your lab:
- transparent tape
- metal contacts*
- battery holder*
- one size D (1.5-volt) battery
- scissors
- copper wire*
- small piece of sandpaper
- light bulb*
- bulb holder*

*included in this kit

STEPS

1. Tape one metal contact to each side of the battery holder (see illustration) and insert the battery into the holder. *Make sure that there is no tape covering the top part of the contacts. Also, be sure that the middle round section on each end of the battery is firmly touching the contact.*

   Use tape to attach contacts.

2. Use your scissors to cut two 8-inch (20-cm) sections of copper wire. Then use the sandpaper to strip 1 inch (2.5 cm) of the plastic coating off the ends of both wires. When you're done, each wire should have a 1-inch (2.5-cm) bare section at each end. *(Note: You will use this battery assembly for some of the other experiments in this book.)*

3. Attach each wire to a metal contact by inserting it through the small hole at the top of the contact and firmly twisting it closed.

4. If your light bulb and holder aren't already connected, attach them by screwing them together tightly.

5. Lay the loose end of one wire in the deep groove above the battery holder, making sure the bare end of the wire lies underneath the bulb hole. Insert the bulb and holder into the hole as shown below, pressing them down firmly onto the wire. Lay the loose end of the other wire in the shallow groove so it touches the top of the bulb holder. What happens?

Conclusion

The battery generates enough power to make your bulb light up dimly but not fully.

Battery

Bulb in holder

Wires

Deep groove

Shallow groove

Traveling the Circuit

When you completed Experiment #4, you probably noticed that the bulb did not light up when you touched it with just one wire. You had to carefully hold two wires against the bulb to bring it to life. That's because an electrical current always travels in a *circuit,* or continuous path. When a complete path, or *closed circuit,* is provided between negative and positive terminals, electrons flow. But when the circuit is *open* (broken), the electrons are unable to jump the gap. They stay where they are and no current is produced.

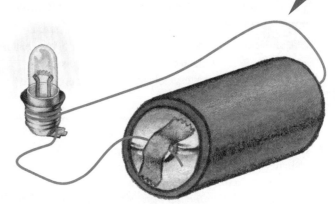

A closed circuit allows electrons to travel in a continuous path.

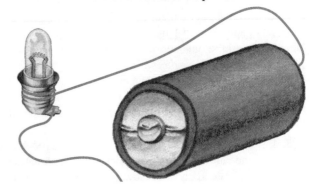

When a circuit is open (unconnected at one or more points) electrons cannot travel.

Remember the example given earlier of rocks in a stream? Imagine now that the rocks stop halfway across the stream. You can't reach the opposite shore from the last rock. That's what happens to electrons when the circuit is open. The electrons can't reach the next atom, so they stop moving forward and the current stops flowing.

In a simple circuit like the one you have just made, the current leaves the energy source (in this case, a battery) and travels down through one wire, through the electrical device (the light bulb), up through the other wire, and back into the battery.

Experiment #5: Make a Switch

How can you show that electricity travels in a circuit?

Set-up

Prepare your lab:
- light bulb*
- bulb holder*
- battery assembly from Experiment #4
- scissors
- copper wire*
- small piece of sandpaper
- metal (uncoated) paper clip

*included in this kit

STEPS

1. First, make sure that the light bulb and bulb holder are screwed tightly together. Then wrap the stripped end of one copper wire from the battery assembly around the top part of the bulb holder. Wrap *tightly* to ensure a good connection.
2. Cut a 6-inch (15-cm) piece of copper wire and use the sandpaper to carefully strip a 1-inch (2.5-cm) section at each end. Lay one of the bare ends in the deep groove. Then insert the bulb and holder into the hole on top of the wire, pressing them down firmly.
3. At this point, you should have two loose wire ends. Insert each loose end through one of the "X's" in the battery holder as shown so that about 1 inch (2.5 cm) of wire sticks up through each hole.
4. Wrap one of the wires firmly around one end of the paper clip.
5. Push the paper clip over so it touches the other wire, then push it away again so it loses contact with the wire. What happens?

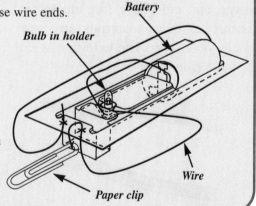

Battery

Bulb in holder

Wire

Paper clip

Conclusion

When the paper clip touches both wires, the circuit is complete, or closed. Electrical current is produced and the bulb lights up. When you break the circuit, or open it, by moving the clip away from one wire, no current flows and the bulb does not light up.

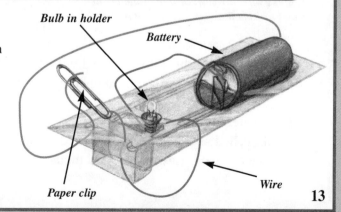

Bulb in holder

Battery

Paper clip

Wire

13

Conductivity

Electricity can't travel in just any old circuit. The circuit must be made of a special material called a *conductor.*

You already know that an electrical current is created when electrons travel from atom to atom. But this motion can only take place with atoms that have "free" electrons (electrons that are not tightly bound to the nucleus). The atoms in materials such as copper, aluminum, silver, and gold have free electrons. Therefore, these materials are very good conductors. The wire in this kit is made from copper.

Most coins are good conductors.

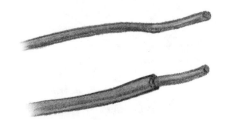

Many wires are covered with insulators to protect us from the electrical current in the wire.

Some materials, called *insulators,* have their atoms so tightly bound together that the outer electrons cannot escape—even when an electrical force is applied. Rubber and glass are two common insulators. Because no current can pass through these materials, they are often used to stop the flow of electricity. The wire in this kit is covered with an insulator. That's why you had to strip the ends of your wire with sandpaper before you could make it do anything.

A few materials are neither good insulators nor good conductors. These materials, called *semiconductors,* are used to make some of the microchips found in computers, televisions, radios, and thousands of other electronic devices.

Experiment #6: Complete the Circuit

What types of materials conduct electricity?

Set-up

Prepare your lab:
• switch assembly from Experiment #5
• various household items, such as keys, toothpicks, coins, straws,
  aluminum foil, or anything else you want to test for conductivity

STEPS

1. Remove the paper clip from your switch assembly. Leave the two wire ends poking up through the holes in the battery holder (make sure the ends don't touch each other).
2. One by one, touch the household items to both wires as shown. Does the bulb light up? Record your answers in the chart below.

Item	Bulb lights?
Paper clip	☑ Yes ❏ No
	❏ Yes ❏ No
	❏ Yes ❏ No
	❏ Yes ❏ No
	❏ Yes ❏ No
	❏ Yes ❏ No
	❏ Yes ❏ No
	❏ Yes ❏ No

Battery

Bulb in holder

Wires

Conclusion

Items that are good conductors complete the circuit and allow an electrical current to travel, lighting up the bulb. Electricity cannot travel through items that act as insulators, so the bulb does not light up when you touch the wires with these items.

Resistance

It is easier for electricity to flow through some conductors than through others. That's because the atoms in some materials are bound more loosely than those in other materials. The looser the bond, the less *resistance* the conductor offers to the flow of electricity. For example, a loosely bound material such as copper offers very little resistance and therefore is a good conductor. A tightly bound material such as lead offers a great deal of resistance, making it difficult for the current to flow.

Resistance is also influenced by a conductor's length and diameter. Long, thin conductors have more resistance than short, thick conductors.

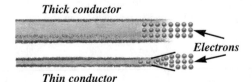

A light dimmer *(rheostat)* works on the principle of resistance. When you turn the dimmer knob, a metal contact inside the rheostat moves against a resistant material. As more of the resistant material becomes part of the circuit, the current traveling through the circuit decreases, and the bulb grows dim.

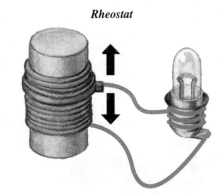

As the ring moves up and down, the resistance of the circuit increases and decreases.

A few special materials called *superconductors* have no resistance at all. Once electricity begins to flow through a superconductor, it just keeps going. But superconductors must be kept extremely cold—about −460°F (−269°C)—to work properly. Because this condition is difficult to produce outside a laboratory, superconductors are not often used in everyday life.

Experiment #7: Make a Rheostat

Does a pencil resist the flow of electricity?

Set-up

Prepare your lab:
• wooden pencil

• screwdriver or
   sharp knife

• the circuit test
   assembly from
   Experiment #6

STEPS

1. Ask an adult to help you prepare the pencil for this
   experiment. First, break the eraser end off the
   pencil. Then have the adult use the screwdriver
   to split the pencil lengthwise down the middle so that the
   graphite is exposed. *(Hint: You can also use a sharp knife to split the pencil—a knife
   may be less likely to slip. But whether you use a screwdriver or a knife, be very
   careful!)* If necessary, rub the graphite gently with sandpaper to remove wood
   fragments.

   Pencil split in half

2. Pull the wires from the circuit test assembly out of the holes.
3. Wrap the bare end of one wire from the circuit test
   assembly around the sharpened end of the pencil.
   Be sure that the bare part of the wire is in firm
   contact with the pencil lead.

   *Wire wrapped around
   pencil point*

4. Touch the bare end of the other wire to the exposed
   graphite near the pencil's sharpened end. What happens?
5. Slide the wire up and down the graphite, making sure it remains in firm contact at all
   times. What happens when the distance between the wire and the sharpened end of
   the pencil changes?

Conclusion

The bulb glows brightly when the two
wire contacts are held close together.
As the distance between the contacts
increases and more of the graphite
becomes part of the circuit, electrical
resistance increases, and the bulb dims.

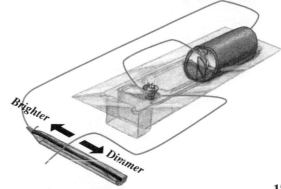

Electrical Heat and Light

When electrons encounter resistance, they give up energy in the form of heat and light. That's why wire sometimes gets hot when it is conducting a current.

Light bulbs work because of resistance. These devices contain a thin, extremely resistant *filament*. As the electrons flow through the filament, they encounter the resistance and release energy—so much so that the filament becomes hot and begins to glow, giving off light.

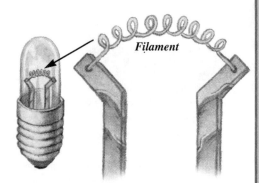

Another very common resistance-based device is a *fuse*. Fuses help make sure that an electrical current doesn't flow too strongly. These small devices contain materials that let current flow freely at normal strength. But if the current becomes too powerful, it burns up the thin wires within the fuse, breaking the circuit so that electricity can no longer flow. Although fuses were once used widely in homes, today they are more often put to work inside small electronic devices.

The filament in a light bulb glows when current travels through it.

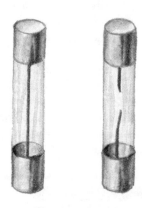

Too much electrical current causes the thin wire in a fuse to burn up and break.

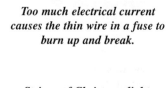

Strings of Christmas lights contain small fuses.

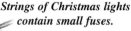

Experiment #8: Sparks in the Dark

How can you use resistance to produce light and heat?

Set-up

Prepare your lab:
• battery assembly from Experiment #7
• metal file (a metal nail file will work well)

STEPS

This experiment is most spectacular in the dark, so find a place away from bright lights before you begin.

1. Disconnect the wire from the pencil in the battery assembly. You should now have two loose wire ends.
2. Wrap the stripped end of one wire from the battery assembly tightly around one end of the metal file.
3. Scrape the stripped end of the loose wire up and down the file. What happens?

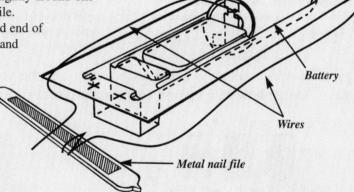

Battery

Wires

Metal nail file

Conclusion

There are lots of little iron filings on the surface of the file. When current flows through these small filings, resistance causes them to give off heat and light, and you can see the sparks fly!

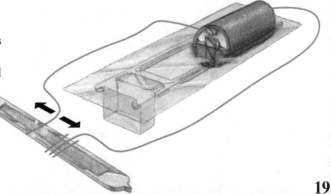

19

Series and Parallel

So far you have made only circuits in which one power source is connected to one device. But several power sources and devices may all be connected in one circuit. The way they are connected can change the behavior of the circuit.

All the parts in a *series circuit* are connected in one circular path. The voltage (amount of electrical pressure) of a series circuit increases as more power sources are connected.

Three 1.5-volt batteries connected in series act as a single battery producing 4.5 volts.

Several devices can be connected in series to a single power source, but each device receives only a fraction of the total power.

A *parallel circuit* is connected in such a way that the voltage is always the same, no matter how many power sources and devices are in the circuit.

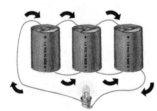

Three batteries connected in parallel produce the same amount of electricity as one battery, but they last much longer than if each was working by itself.

Two bulbs connected in parallel to one battery would each receive the full 1.5 volts. But they would use up the battery's power very quickly.

Parallel circuits are practical for everyday use because if one device or power source fails, the circuit will remain unbroken for the rest of the items. A series circuit is broken as soon as any portion of it is removed.

Experiment #9: Brighter and Dimmer

What happens to a light bulb when you connect two batteries to it in series or in parallel?

 Set-up

Prepare your lab:
• battery assembly from Experiment #8
• scissors
• copper wire*
• small piece of sandpaper

• transparent tape
• one size D (1.5-volt) battery
  (in addition to the one in the battery assembly)
• light bulb*
• bulb holder*

included in this kit

STEPS

1. Disconnect the wire from the file in the battery assembly. You should now have two loose wire ends.
2. Cut a 6-inch (15-cm) piece of copper wire. Use the sandpaper to strip a 1-inch (2.5-cm) section at each end of the wire. You will also use the 6-inch (15-cm) section of wire you prepared for Experiment #5.
3. Use transparent tape to attach the four wires to a second battery in parallel as shown. Note that the wire from the first battery's negative (–) terminal must run to the second battery's negative terminal, and the wire from the positive (+) terminal must run to the battery's positive terminal.
4. Lay the loose end of one wire in the plastic frame's deep groove and insert the bulb and holder (they should be tightly screwed together) so they sit on top of the wire. Lay the loose end of the other wire in the shallow groove so it touches the top of the bulb holder. What happens?
5. Remove the tape from both ends of the second battery to disconnect all the wires. Reconnect them in series, as shown. Note that the wire from the first battery's negative terminal must run to the second battery's positive terminal.
6. Insert the wires and bulb into the hole, as you did in Step 3. What happens now?

Conclusion

When the batteries are connected in parallel the bulb glows, but only dimly. When the batteries are connected in series the bulb glows much more brightly.

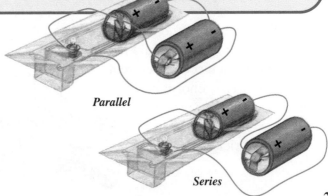

Parallel

Series

Electricity and Magnetism

You have read a bit about heat and light, two important effects of electricity. Another important effect is *magnetism*. Whenever an electrical current flows, a magnetic field is produced.

Even a single thin wire produces a weak magnetic field. But this field can be increased by coiling the wire. The more loops of wire there are in the coil, the stronger the magnetic field will be. A coiled wire is called a *solenoid*.

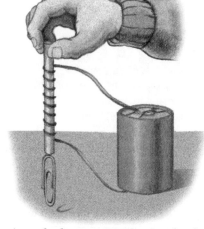

If you insert a piece of metal through a solenoid, the metal will be temporarily magnetized when a current is run through it. This type of magnet is referred to as an *electromagnet* because it is activated by electricity. Telephones contain small electromagnets. So do doorbells. And you may have seen pictures of the giant electromagnets used in junkyards to separate metal from other materials. These powerful magnets are strong enough to lift a car!

A regular battery can turn a metal rod into an electromagnet.

Some electromagnets are powerful enough to lift cars.

Magnetism can also produce electricity. When a solenoid spins rapidly between two magnets, an electrical current is created. The enormous generators that power our cities use this method to produce electricity.

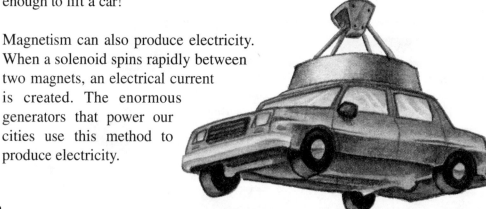

Experiment #10: Go with the Flow

How can you show that an electrical current produces magnetism?

Set-up *Prepare your lab:*
- small piece of sandpaper
- copper wire*
- metal rod*
- series assembly from Experiment #9
- small magnetic compass

*included in this kit

STEPS

1. Use the sandpaper to strip 1 inch (2.5 cm) of coating off the ends of the remaining piece of copper wire, which should be about 15 inches (38 cm) long.
2. Wrap the wire tightly around the metal rod, as shown, forming a solenoid. When you're finished, pull the metal rod out and set it aside. Leave the bare ends of the wire sticking out from the solenoid.
3. Connect one wire from the solenoid to one of the free ends of the series assembly.
4. Set the compass on a flat surface with the dial facing up. With one finger, gently hold the solenoid down so it lies on top of the compass.
5. Touch the free wire from the solenoid to the free wire from the series assembly to create a circuit. What happens to the compass dial when electrical current flows?

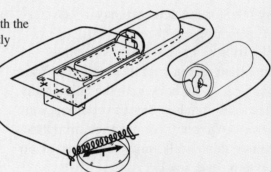

Conclusion

Compasses are designed to read magnetic fields. The compass dial moves when current flows above it, showing that an electrical current is magnetic. When the current stops flowing, the compass dial returns to its original position.

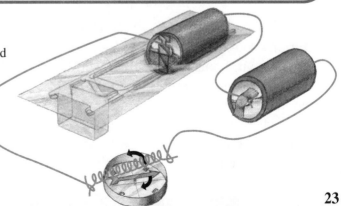

23

Electricity and You

Through simple experiments, you've found out about the exciting world of electricity. You now understand how electricity is generated and how it flows through conductors. And you've seen how light bulbs, switches, batteries, and many other everyday objects work.

By now, you probably realize that electricity does much more than just turn on our lights. It is crucial in almost every aspect of our lives. In fact, learning to harness electricity was one of the most important scientific advancements ever made. Without electrical power, we couldn't run our cars, watch TV, use computers, or do most of the other things we take for granted each day.

Without electricity we couldn't watch our favorite programs on TV.

Electricity in nature also plays an important role in your everyday life. Your brain runs your body with the help of tiny electrical impulses that travel along your nerves. Without these electrical impulses, you couldn't walk, talk, see, hear, or do anything else at all!

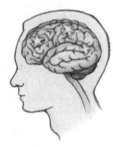

Your brain generates tiny electrical impulses.

Now that you know so much about electricity, look for examples of how it's used in your home and in the world around you. You can even make up new experiments using the components in this book. Get creative! But most of all, have fun as you embark on your *electrifying* journey of discovery!

Electrical lamps light our homes.